International code of nomenclature for cultivated plants-1980

Formulated and adopted by the International Commission for the Nomenclature of Cultivated Plants of the I.U.B.S.
Edited by C.D. Brickell, chairman, E.G. Voss, A.F. Kelly, F. Schneider, members, R.H. Richens, secretary of the Editorial Committee

1980
Bohn, Scheltema & Holkema, Utrecht
dr. W. Junk b.v., Publishers, The Hague

Obtainable from:

THE INTERNATIONAL BUREAU FOR PLANT TAXONOMY AND NOMENCLA-TURE, Tweede Transitorium, Uithof, Utrecht, Netherlands.
THE AMERICAN HORTICULTURAL SOCIETY, Mt. Vernon, Virginia 22121, USA
CROP SCIENCE SOCIETY OF AMERICA, 677 South Segoe Road, Madison, Wisconsin 53711, USA
THE ROYAL HORTICULTURAL SOCIETY, Vincent Square, London, SW1P 2PE, Great Britain.

Correspondence concerning this Code and the work of the International Commission for the Nomenclature of Cultivated Plants, proposals for the future amendment of the Code and requests for information on Cultivar Registration Authorities should be addressed to the present Secretary of the Commission, Mr. F. Schneider, Afd. Botanisch Onderzoek Tuinbouwgewassen, RIVRO, Wageningen, Netherlands.

PREFACE

The last edition of the International Code for the Nomenclature of Cultivated Plants (abbreviated in common usage to Cultivated Code) was published in 1969 (Regnum Vegetabile Vol. 64, pp. 32).

The last ten years have seen the question of cultivar nomenclature rising steadily in importance, largely because of the various international and national measures in operation to protect buyers of plant material and to provide for plant breeders' rights. The International Commission for the Nomenclature of Cultivated Plants, whose various editions of the Cultivated Code have provided the main scientific background now embodied in cultivar-name legislation, is glad to note how closely the Cultivated Code and corresponding legislation are in accord and is glad also that the hope expressed in the preface of the 1969 Cultivated Code, that the edition then produced would be adequate for the following decade, has been fulfilled. The articles in the 1969 Code were re-arranged and re-numbered to improve their logical sequence and ease of consultation, but the hope was recorded that the new arrangement might prove adequate even through subsequent amendment. The Commission has found that this is indeed so, and the arrangement and numbering of the articles conform exactly with those of the previous edition.

Though a great many detailed changes have been made in the text of the present edition, largely to clarify meaning or add examples, the overall text is very similar to that of the 1969 edition. The principal changes are as follows:

1. A clearer distinction is drawn between cultivar names and trade-marks applied to cultivars, and between cultivar registration and registration of trade-marks which may be applied to cultivars (Arts. 3, 4, 53, 56).

2. It is explicity stated that a cultivar may, on occasion, be co-extensive with the botanical category under which it is classified (Art. 10).

3. A forestry provenance, when sufficiently distinctive, may be treated as a cultivar (Art. 10).

4. Particular growth-habit forms which are retained by appropriate methods of propagation are treated as cultivars (Art. 11).

5. Segregates of interspecific or intergeneric crosses resembling one parent in nearly all its characters are classified under this parent, not under the hybrid combination (Art. 13).

6. The formula designating somatic hybrids is expressed using the multiplication sign within parentheses (round braçkets) (Art. 14).

7. Latin cultivar names derived from botanical epithets published before 1 January 1959 are regarded as validly published as long as they are in conformity with the present Code (Art. 27).

8. The different significance of a botanical varietal epithet in italics and the same epithet in Roman type used for a cultivar and typographically distinguished is spelled out and exemplified (Art. 27).

9. The various approved ways of printing cultivar names are set out in greater detail (Art. 29).

10. It is strongly recommended that cultivar names should not incorporate the common name of the plant (Art. 31A).

11. Chinese, Japanese and Korean books are considered validly published when reproduced from a hand-written original, irrespective of date (Art. 37).

12. Conditions for re-use of cultivar names are made more stringent (Art. 48).

Appendix II of the 1969 Code has been omitted since there has been no re-numbering of articles and recommendations in the current revision.

The early history of Codes for the nomenclature of cultivated plants was outlined by Dr. W. T. Stearn in his historical introduction to the 1953 Code (Royal Horticultural Society, London: Pp. 29).

The 1953 Code was drawn up by the International Botanical Congress Committee for the Nomenclature of Cultivated Plants and the International Commission for Horticultural Nomenclature and Registration at the Thirteenth International Horticultural Congress, London, September, 1952.

The International Commission for the Nomenclature of Cultivated Plants of the International Union of Biological Sciences was responsible for the next edition of the Cultivated Code. The Commission had been enlarged after the Fourteenth International Horticultural Congress held at Scheveningen, Netherlands, in 1955, and held its first meeting at Utrecht, Netherlands, in November 1956, to revise and expand the 1953 Code to make it applicable to agriculture and forestry as well as horticulture. The enlarged Commission consisted of approximately equal numbers of members representing agriculture, horticulture, and forestry. The members representing agriculture were appointed after consultation with the Food and Agriculture Organization of the United Nations, the members representing forestry after consultation with the International Union of Forest Research Organizations, and the members representing horticulture on the nomination of the International Commission for Horticultural Nomenclature and Registration of the International Society for Horticultural Science. The task of revision was completed at the next meeting of the Commission at London, England, in December 1957, and the outcome was the 1958 Code (*Regnum Vegetabile*, Vol. 10, Pp. 28).

A further meeting of the Commission took place at Cambridge, England, in June 1960. Only relatively minor changes in the Code were adopted at this meeting, and these were embodied in the 1961 Code.

Work on the preceding edition of the Code began in August 1964, when the Commission met at Edinburgh, Scotland. It met again at College Park, Maryland, USA, in August 1966, and the main work of collating proposals began in the autumn of 1968.

The Commission met to draw up the 1969 edition of the Code in Cambridge, England, in February 1969. This meeting was preceded by an Open Meeting attended by representatives of commercial firms, professional organizations and government departments concerned with cultivar (variety) names.

In October 1979, when the present edition of the Code was prepared, the Commission consisted of the following members:

Chairman

Mr. C.D. Brickell, Royal Horticultural Society, Wisley, Woking, Surrey, England.

Secretary

Dr. R.H. Richens, Commonwealth Bureau of Plant Breeding & Genetics, Cambridge, England.

Agricultural Representatives:

Dr. D.C. Giacometti, Empresa Brasileira de Pesquisa Agropecuária, Avenida W-5 Norte Parque Rural, Brasil.

Prof. J.G. Hawkes, Dept. of Plant Biology, University of Birmingham, PO. Box 363, Birmingham, B15 2TT, England.

Mr. A.F. Kelly, National Institute of Agricultural Botany, Cambridge, England.

Dr. J. León, CATIE, Apartado 102, Turrialba, Costa Rica.

Dr. B.P. Pal, Indian Agricultural Research Institute, New Delhi, India.

Prof. D.J. Rogers, Dept. EPO Biology, University of Colorado, Boulder, Colo. 80309, USA.

Dr. M.S. Swaminathan, Indian Council of Agricultural Research, Prishi Bhavan, Dr. Rajendra Prasad Road, New Delhi, India.

Dr. Martin G. Weiss, 11122 Emack Road, Beltsville, Md. 20705, USA.

Forestry Representatives:

Dr. W.B. Critchfield, Pacific Southwest Forest and Range Experiment Station, PO Box 245, Berkeley, California 95701, USA.

Dr. S. Herrmann, Institut für Forstgenetik und Forstpflanzenzüchtung, 207 Schmalenbeck über Ahrensberg, German Federal Republic.

Dr. R.D. Johnston, CSIRO Division of Forest Research, Canberra, Australia.

Mr. A.F. Mitchell, Forest Research Station, Alice Holt Lodge, Wrecclesham, Farnham, Surrey, England.

Mr. J. Pourtet, Direction Générale des Forêts, 1 ter Avenue Lowendal, Paris 7e, France.

Prof. R.S. Ramalho, Departmento de Engenharia Florestal Universidade Federal de Viçosa, Viçosa MG36570 Brazil.

Dr. B.T. Styles, Commonwealth Forestry Institute, Oxford, England.

Dr. R. Toda, Forestry and Forest Products Research Institute, 300-12 Usika PO Box 2, Ibaraki, Japan.

Horticultural Representatives:

Dr. William J. Dress, Bailey Hortorium, Cornell University, Ithaca, New York 14853, USA.

Prof. R. Maatsch, Institut für Zierpflanzenbau der Technischen Universität Hannover-Herrenhausen, Herrenhäuder Str. 2, German Federal Republic.

Mr. F. Schneider, Afd. Botanisch Onderzoek Tuinbouwgewassen, RIVRO, Wageningen, Netherlands.

Dr. S.A. Spongberg, Arnold Arboretum, 22 Divinity Avenue, Cambridge, Mass. 02138, USA.

Mr. F.Vrugtman,Royal Botanical Gardens, Box 339, Hamilton, Canada, L8N 3H8.

Representative of the International Union of Biological Sciences

Dr. E.G. Voss, University of Michigan Herbarium, Ann Arbor, Michigan, 48109, USA.

Proposals for amendments to the previous edition of the Code were received from 1969 onwards. These were collated and sent to Commission members in June 1979, and these proposals and subsequent comments received on them were considered at a Plenary Meeting of the Commission held at the National Institute of Agricultural Botany, Cambridge, England, during 1-3 October 1979. At this meeting, the form that amendments to the Code should take was agreed in principle and the final drafting of the present edition was entrusted to the Commission's Editorial Committee. The Commission wishes to record its thanks to all individuals who submitted proposals to amend the Code; all these were carefully considered by the Commission when reaching its conclusions.

Lastly, I would like to record both personally and on behalf of the Commission and its Editorial Committee, our warmest thanks to the retiring Secretary, Dr. R.H. Richens, not only for the immense amount of time he has devoted to preparations for the Commission meetings at Cambridge, but for the very clear and valuable guidance he provided during the meetings and in the drafting of the text of this new edition.

All past and present members of the Commission will, I am certain, join with me in extending their warmest thanks to the previous Chairman, J.S.L. Gilmour, whose contributions to the nomenclature of cultivated plants, in general, and to this Code, in particular, have been of immeasurable value.

The present (1980) edition, drawn up at the Plenary Meeting of the Commission mentioned above, becomes effective from the date of its publication.

C.D. Brickell,
Chairman of the Commission and of
the Editorial Committee

INTERNATIONAL CODE OF NOMENCLATURE FOR CULTIVATED PLANTS 1980

General Considerations and Guiding Principles

Article 1

Cultivated plants are essential to civilization. It is important, therefore, that a precise, stable, and internationally accepted system should be available for their naming.

Article 2

The *International Code of Botanical Nomenclature* (Botanical Code)* governs the use of botanical names in Latin form for both cultivated and wild plants, except for graft-chimaeras (see Arts. 20–24).

Article 3

The aim of the present Code (Cultivated Code) is to promote uniformity, accuracy, and fixity in the naming of agricultural, horticultural, and silvicultural cultivars (varieties) (see Arts. 5, 10, and 11), which are normally given fancy names, such as apple 'Cox's Orange Pippin', barley 'Proctor', *Juglans regia* 'King'.

A cultivar name must be freely available for use by any person to denote the cultivar (variety) whose name it is. In certain countries, trade-marks are also attached to cultivars (varieties). They may only be used in conformity with trade-mark law. The same trade-mark may, in some countries, be attached to different cultivars (varieties), and, in some countries also, the same trade-mark may be attached not only to cultivars but to other objects. A cultivar name cannot, in general, be registered as a trade-mark.

The common names of genera and species, such as beech for *Fagus*, potato for *Solanum tuberosum*, hollyhock for *Alcea rosea*, Jerusalem artichoke for *Helianthus tuberosus*, and rye for *Secale*, are not regulated by this Code.

Article 4

Registration of cultivar (variety) names is of the greatest importance for nomenclatural stability (see Arts. 53–56 and Appendix).

Registration of trade-marks which may be applied to cultivars is a legal process and is not the concern of this Code.

Article 5

Cultivar (variety) names are also used in enactments having the force of national or international law. This Code has no force beyond that deriving from the free assent of those concerned with cultivated plants. It is, however, strongly urged that the Articles and Recommendations of this Code be accepted and applied by all those responsible for the legal use of cultivar (variety) names.

Article 6

The Articles of this Code are retroactive except when expressly limited (see Arts. 27, 30, 31, 34, 37–39, 44, 45, 55).

* Current edition: F.A. Stafleu *et al.* International Code of Botanical Nomenclature, adopted by the Twelfth International Botanical Congress, Leningrad, July 1975, *Regnum Vegetabile* Vol. 97, Pp. 457, 1978.

11

CATEGORIES AND THEIR DESIGNATIONS

Main Categories

Article 7

Cultivated plants are named at three main levels: genus, species, and cultivar (variety).

Article 8

Names at the genus (generic) level are:

a. Botanical generic names and common names used in a generic sense (*Lilium, Pinus, Triticum,* lily, pine, wheat).

b. Botanical and common names of intergeneric hybrids (×*Triticosecale,* ×*Sorbopyrus,* ×*Sanderara,* triticale).

c. Botanical and common names of intergeneric graft-chimaeras (+*Crataegomespilus*).

Article 9

Names at the species (specific) level are:

a. Botanical and common names of species (*Lilium candidum,* Madonna lily).

b. Botanical and common names of interspecific hybrids (*Tilia* ×*vulgaris,* common lime).

c. Botanical and common names of interspecific graft-chimaeras (*Syringa* +*correlata*).

d. Botanical and common names of particular interspecific combinations of an intergeneric hybrid (×*Cupressocyparis leylandii*; citrange).

Note. The botanical specific name is a binary combination (binomial) consisting of the name of the genus followed by a single specific epithet.

Example: *Lilium candidum,* where *Lilium* is the generic name and *candidum* the specific epithet.

Article 10

The international term *cultivar* denotes an assemblage of cultivated plants which is clearly distinguished by any characters (morphological, physiological, cytological, chemical, or others), and which, when reproduced (sexually or asexually), retains its distinguishing characters.

The cultivar is the lowest category under which names are recognized in this Code. This term is derived from *culti*vated *vari*ety, or their etymological equivalents in other languages.

Note 1. Mode of origin is irrelevant when considering whether two populations belong to the same or to different cultivars.

Examples: Carnation 'William Sim' produces colour mutants which by further mutation and back mutation give rise to indistinguishable colour variants of diverse origin. All indistinguishable colour variants, irrespective of their origin, are treated as one cultivar. The tobaccos described as 'MacNair 30' and 'NC 2326' constitute only one cultivar since, though they derived their resistance to *Phytophthora parasitica* var. *nicotianae* from different wild species, they cannot be distinguished by their present characters.

Note 2. The concept of cultivar is essentially different from the concept of botanical variety, *varietas*. The latter is a category below that of species. Names of botanical varieties are always in Latin form and are governed by the Botanical Code. Rules for the formation of cultivar names are set out in the present Code (see Arts. 27–32).

Note 3. The term cultivar is equivalent to *variety* in English, *variété* in French, *variedad* in Spanish, *variedade* in Portuguese, *varietà* or *razza* in Italian, *varieteit* or *ras* in Dutch, *Sorte* in German, *sort* in Scandinavian languages and Russian, *pinzhong (p'in-chung)* in Chinese, and *hinshu* in Japanese, whenever these words are used to denote a cultivated variety.

Note 4. The terms cultivar and variety (in the sense of cultivated variety) are exact equivalents. In translations or adaptations of the Code for special purposes either *cultivar* or *variety* (or its equivalent in other languages) may be used in the text.

Note 5. Usually a cultivar will comprise a part only of the species, botanical variety or other botanical category under which it is classified. A cultivar may however be co-extensive with any of these.

Note 6. When a forestry provenance is clearly distinguished by one or more characters and, when reproduced, retains its distinguishing characters, it may be treated as a cultivar.

Article 11

Cultivars differ in their modes of reproduction. The following are examples of categories that can be distinguished:

a. A cultivar consisting of one clone or several closely similar clones. A clone is a genetically uniform assemblage of individuals (which may be chimaeral in nature), derived originally from a single individual by asexual propagation, for example by cuttings, divisions, grafts, or obligate apomixis. Individuals propagated from a distinguishable bud-mutation form a cultivar distinct from the parent plant.

Examples: *Fraxinus excelsior* 'Westhof's Glorie'; potato 'Bintje'; *Cynodon dactylon* 'Coastal'; *Syringa vulgaris* 'Decaisne'; *Rubus nitidoides* 'Merton Early'.

b. A cultivar consisting of one or more similar lines of normally self-fertilizing individuals or inbred lines of normally cross-fertilizing individuals.

Examples: *Triticum aestivum* 'Marquis'; *Zea mays* 'Wisconsin 153A'.

Note. A multiline composite variety may be treated as a single cultivar or as a mixture of different cultivars.

c. A cultivar consisting of cross-fertilized individuals which may show genetical differences but having one or more characters by which it can be differentiated from other cultivars.

Examples: *Lolium perenne* 'Scotia'; *Phlox drummondii* 'Sternenzauber', a mixture of different colour forms, all characterized by the same star-like shape of the corolla; *Medicago sativa* 'Ranger', the breeder seed of which is derived from intercrossing five seed-propagated lines, each maintained under isolation.

d. A cultivar consisting of an assemblage of individuals reconstituted on each occasion by crossing. This includes single-crosses, double-crosses, three-way crosses, top-crosses, and intervarietal (intercultivar) hybrids.

Examples: Sorghum 'Texas 610', a single cross; maize 'US 13', a double-cross involving four inbred lines; maize 'H-611', an intervarietal hybrid of 'Kenya Flat White' and 'Ecuador 573'.

e. A cultivar consisting of one clone or several closely similar clones which have a habit of growth which is clearly distinguishable from the normal habit and which is retained by appropriate methods of propagation.

Examples: *Chamaecyparis pisifera* 'Squarrosa Intermedia', a juvenile form; *Sequoia sempervirens* 'Prostrata', a prostrate form; *Picea abies* 'Pygmaea', a witches' broom.

Article 12

The practice of designating a selection of a cultivar as a strain or equivalent term is

13

not adopted in this Code. Any such selection showing sufficient differences from the parent cultivar to render it worthy of a name is to be regarded as a distinct cultivar (see Rec. 12A).

Note. The term "strain", in addition to its usual sense indicated above, is sometimes used, as in lilies, for a cultivar group of hybrid origin, for example *Lilium* Olympic strain. The usage recommended by this Code for groups is set out in Arts. 25 and 26.

Recommendation 12A.

A new cultivar which originated by selection or by bud-mutation from another cultivar, and which still retains a strong resemblance to it, should, when appropriate, but not in any way that could cause confusion, be named to indicate the relationship. The same applies to new cultivars differentiated by the introduction of a single character.

Examples: Apple 'Crimson Bramley' is a bud-mutant from apple 'Bramley's Seedling'; cabbage 'Wisconsin All Seasons', resitant to the disease "yellows", is a selection from the nonresistant cabbage 'All Seasons'; soya bean 'Amsoy 71', resitant to *Phytophthora sojae*, was derived by outcrossing to a resitant type and repeated back crossing to 'Amsoy'.

Collective Names

Note 1. A collective name is the single designation covering all the progeny of a particular hybrid combination.

Note 2. Arts. 13–17 are based on the Arts. H. 1–10 of the Botanical Code.

Article 13.

Botanical names in Latin form for interspecific and intergeneric hybrids and their derivatives are governed by the Botanical Code. Such hybrids are designated either by a formula or by a name. All derivatives from the combination of the same two or more parental species have the same formula or the same botanical name except where established custom or special circumstances demand otherwise, as, for example, in hybrids of different chromosome status.

Where, however, a hybrid segregate resembles one parent only in nearly all characters, it is given the same name as that parent.

Article 14.

The formula designating first and subsequent generations of an interspecific or intergeneric cross consists of the botanical names of the parents connected by the multiplication sign, ×.

Examples: The formula for all interspecific cultivars derived from crosses involving *Camellia japonica* and *C. saluenensis* is *Camellia japonica* × *C. saluenensis*. A particular cultivar of this parentage, for example 'Donation', may be designated (*Camellia japonica* × *C. saluenensis*) 'Donation'. The formula for all cultivars derived from intergeneric crosses involving *Festuca pratensis* and *Lolium perenne* is *Festuca pratensis* × *Lolium perenne*. A particular cultivar of this parentage, for example 'Prior', may be designated (*Festuca pratensis*) × *Lolium perenne* 'Prior'.

The formula designating derivatives of an interspecific or intergeneric somatic cross, obtained by a parasexual process such as protoplast fusion, consists of the botanical names of the parents connected by the multiplication sign within parentheses (round brackets).

Example: *Nicotiana glauca* (×) *Nicotiana langsdorffii*.

Recommendation 14A

The order of the names may be either alphabetical (as in this Code), or, when the female parent is known, with the name of the female parent first. The male (♂) and female (♀) signs may be added if desired. The method used in any publication should be clearly stated.

Article 15

The botanical name designating first and subsequent generations of an interspecific cross consists of the generic name followed by a Latin collective epithet, the latter immediately preceded by the multiplication sign, ×.

Examples: All hybrid cultivars derived from the crossing of *Camellia japonica* and *C. saluenensis* may be designated by the collective name in Latin form *Camellia ×williamsii*. A particular cultivar, for example 'Donation', may be cited as *Camellia ×williamsii* 'Donation', or merely *Camellia* 'Donation'. *Lilium ×sulphurgale* is the collective name for hybrids between *Lilium regale* and *L. sulphureum*.

Note. The Latin collective epithet of an interspecific hybrid is not affected when the botanical name of either parent is changed for nomenclatural reasons.

Article 16

The botanical name of first and subsequent generations of an intergeneric cross involving two genera consists of a "generic" name, normally formed by a combination of parts of the names of the two parent genera immediately preceded by the multiplication sign, ×, and followed by a Latin collective epithet.

The "generic" name of an intergeneric hybrid involving four or more genera consists of a personal name to which the termination -*ara* is added. The "generic" name of an intergeneric hybrid involving three genera is formed by a combination of parts of the names of the three parent genera, or consists of a personal name to which the termination -*ara* is added.

All derivatives from a particular intergeneric cross, whatever the species, have the same "generic" name.

Example: All progeny derived from the crossing of any *Cupressus* species with any *Chamaecyparis* species may be designated by the collective name in Latin form ×*Cupressocyparis*.

All derivatives from a particular combination of species in an intergeneric cross have the same collective epithet.

Examples: All progeny derived from crosses between *Cupressus macrocarpa* and *Chamaecyparis nootkatensis* may be designated by the collective name in Latin form ×*Cupressocyparis leylandii*. Progeny derived from crosses between *Cupressus glabra* and *Chamaecyparis nootkatensis* may be designated by the collective name ×*Cupressocyparis notabilis*.

×*Potinara* covers all the hybrids derived from the combination *Brassavola* × *Cattleya* × *Laelia* × *Sophronitis*; ×*Wilsonara* covers all the hybrids derived from the combination *Cochlioda* × *Odontoglossum* × *Oncidium*; ×*Sophrolaeliocattleya* covers all the hybrids derived from the combination *Cattleya* × *Laelia* × *Sophronitis*.

Article 17

For valid publication of the botanical "generic" name of an intergeneric hybrid, the names of the parent genera must be stated, but no description or Latin diagnosis is necessary. Such a name is regarded as a condensed formula. For valid publication of a collective epithet in Latin form of an interspecific or intergeneric hybrid, it must, on or after 1 January 1935, have a Latin diagnosis and be placed under a generic name.

Article 18

A collective epithet may also be a word or a phrase of not more than three words in a modern language. For the purposes of this article, an arbitrary sequence of letters, an abbreviation, or a numeral is counted as a word. All derivatives from the combina-

15

tion of the same two or more parental species have the same collective epithet in a modern language except where established custom or special circumstances demand otherwise, as, for example, in orchids.

Recommendation 18A

A phrase used as a collective epithet may contain a word such as Hybrid, Hybrids, Cross, Crosses, grex (abbreviated g., Latin for swarm or flock), etc., indicating the collective nature of the unit.

Example: *Lilium* Bellingham Hybrids is a collective name in modern language for interspecific hybrids between *Lilium humboldtii* and *L. pardalinum*.

Recommendation 18B

A collective epithet in modern language, if it is followed by a cultivar name, should normally be placed in parentheses (round brackets), for example, *Lilium* (Bellingham Hybrids) 'Shuksan', *Rosa* (Hybrid Tea) 'Richmond', *Cattleya* (Fabia g.) 'Prince of Wales'. The parentheses may be omitted, and, in a context where the status of the collective epithet is clear, the word grex or its abbreviation may also be omitted, for example, *Cattleya* Fabia 'Prince of Wales'.

Note. It is not admissible to use the multiplication sign, ×, as part of a collective epithet.

Example: *Lilium* (×Bellingham) 'Shuksan' or *Lilium* (×Bellingham Hybrids) 'Shuksan' should not be used for *Lilium* (Bellingham Hybrids) 'Shuksan'.

Article 19

An interspecific hybrid introduced into cultivation without a cultivar name must be given a cultivar name whenever later material of the same parentage, differing from the first in one or more clearly distinguishable characters, is also introduced.

Example: When the first cultivar of *Viburnum* × *bodnantense* (*V. farreri* × *V. grandiflorum*) was introduced into cultivation, it was not given a cultivar name. In order to distinguish it from other forms of the same parentage which have been produced, the name 'Dawn' was later given to it.

Recommendation 19A

An interspecific hybrid introduced into cultivation without a cultivar name should be given a cultivar name in addition to the collective epithet formula, even if no other cultivar of the hybrid is known.

Graft-Chimaeras

Article 20

Graft-chimaeras are composed of tissues in intimate association from two different plants. They originate by grafting and are not sexual hybrids. Graft-chimaeras are designated by a formula or by a name in Latin form. Such names are validly published by stating the botanical names of the component plants in the publication in which the graft-chimaera is cited. The orthography of words in Latin forms which are used for names of graft-chimaeras should be in accordance with the Botanical Code; if not, the spelling should be corrected.

Article 21

The formula of a graft-chimaera consists of the names of the two components in alphabetical order connected by the addition (plus) sign, +.

Examples: *Cytisus purpureus* + *Laburnum anagyroides; Syringa* ×*chinensis* + *S. vulgaris*.

16

Article 22

When the components of a graft-chimaera belong to the same genus, the name consists of the generic name followed by an addition sign, +, and an epithet. The epithet must not be the same as that of a sexual hybrid between the same species as the components of the graft-chimaera.

Example: *Syringa* + *correlata* (*Syringa* ×*chinensis* + *S. vulgaris*).

Article 23

When the components of a graft-chimaera belong to different genera, the name consists of a new "generic" name normally formed by combining the generic names of the components, preceded by an addition sign, +, and followed by an epithet. The "generic" name and epithet must not be the same as that of a sexual hybrid between the same species as the components of the graft-chimaera.

Examples: +*Crataegomespilus dardarii* (*Crataegus monogyna* + *Mespilus germanica*), but × *Crataemespilus gillottii* (*Crataegus monogyna* × *Mespilus germanica*); +*Laburnocytisus adamii* (*Cytisus purpureus* + *Laburnum anagyroides*).

Article 24

The same two components may build a graft-chimaera in more than one way. These different graft-chimaeras must be designated by the same formula or name but are treated as distinct cultivars.

Examples: +*Crataegomespilus dardarii* 'Bronvaux' and 'Jules d'Asnières'.

Supplementary Categories

Article 25

Supplementary botanical categories are governed by the Botanical Code. Some, such as subgenus, sectio (section), or series, are subdivisions of a genus. The names of such categories, if used, are placed within parentheses (round brackets) immediately after the generic name.

Examples: *Prunus* (subg. *Cerasus*) *avium* 'Erianne'; *Primula* (sect. *Candelabra*) *japonica* 'Postford White'; *Iris* (ser. *Laevigatae*) *laevigata* 'Mottled Beauty'.

Other categories, such as subspecies, varietas (variety), and forma (form), denote subdivisions of a species and, if used, are placed after the specific epithet.

Examples: *Ranunculus acris* subsp. *friesianus* 'Plenus'; *Rosa sericea* var. *omeiensis* 'Praecox'.

Article 26

When a species, interspecific hybrid or intergeneric hybrid includes many cultivars, an assemblage of similar cultivars may be designated as a group. This category is intermediate between species and cultivar. It is not an essential part of the full cultivar name. If used between the specific name or collective name and the cultivar name, the name of the group is placed within parentheses (round brackets).

Examples: *Rhododendron cinnabarinum* Blandfordiiflorum group; *Phaseolus vulgaris* (Dwarf French bean group) 'Masterpiece'; *Rhododendron cinnabarinum* subsp. *xanthocodon* (Concatenans group) 'Copper' or *Rhododendron cinnabarinum* (Concatenans group) 'Copper'; pea (Vining group) 'Sprite'; *Lolium perenne* (Early group) 'Devon Eaver'; maize (200-299 maturity group) 'W240'.

Note. In complex crops, for example, in apples and in some cereals, a hierarchy of categories has been applied, the use of which is not governed by this Code.

17

FORMATION OF CULTIVAR NAMES

Article 27

a. A cultivar name published on or after 1 January 1959, must, except as noted in (b) and (c) below, be a fancy name, that is, not a botanical name in Latin form (see Arts. 30 and 31).

The full name of a cultivar comprises the botanical or common name of the species and the cultivar name. Strictly, the latter element is an epithet and can be referred to as a cultivar epithet for purposes of precision.

Examples: New cultivars introduced on or after 1 January 1959 must not be given names in Latin form such as 'Totus Albus', 'Alba Striata', nor partly in Latin form such as 'Hyemalis Southcote'. However, names of these types given before 1 January 1959, for example, *Hibiscus syriacus* 'Totus Albus', *Hemerocallis* 'Alba Striata', must not be rejected because they are in Latin form.

b. A botanical epithet in Latin form, published in conformity with the Botanical Code, before, on, or after 1 January 1959, or published in conformity with this Code only, before 1 January 1959, for a plant or plants subsequently considered to be a cultivar, is to be retained as a cultivar name unless it duplicates an existing cultivar name of the species or hybrid concerned (see Art. 50).

Examples: *Rhododendron carolinianum* f. *luteum*, published by Frisbie, *J. Arn. Arb. 40:* 156, 1959, when treated as a cultivar co-extensive with this botanical category and not as a form, becomes *Rhododendron carolinianum* 'Luteum'. The plant long cultivated under the name *Nopalxochia ackermannii* is different from the wild species that bears this name which has recently been rediscovered in the wild state. The cultivated plant is, in fact, an interspecific hybrid of the parentage *Heliocereus speciosus* × *Nopalxochia phyllanthoides* and consequently is assignable to × *Heliochia*. It may retain its epithet as × *Heliochia* 'Ackermannii' when treated as a cultivar.

c. When there are two or more previously published botanical epithets in Latin form, the epithet that best preserves established usage should be chosen, without regard to the botanical category in which the epithet was published, or to priority.

Article 28

The orthography of words in Latin form which are used as cultivar names should be in accordance with the Botanical Code; if not, the spelling should be corrected.

Examples: (a) Cultivar names in the genitive singular derived from personal names normally end in -ii (men) or -iae (women), unless the personal name ends in a vowel (including y, and j in certain Slav languages) or in -er, in which case they should end in -i or -ae; thus 'Jonesii', 'Schmidtiae', 'Roylei', 'Cooperi', 'Donckelaarii', 'Roumeyi', 'Alexeji'.

(b) Cultivar names, when adjectival in form, should agree in gender with the generic name concerned: thus, *Begonia* 'Elegantissima Superba', *Rhus typhina* 'Dissecta', *Malus floribunda* 'Arnoldiana', *Hibiscus syriacus* 'Violaceus', *Lilium* × *maculatum* 'Sanguineum', *Calluna vulgaris* 'Carnea'.

Article 29

A cultivar name, when immediately following a botanical or common name, must be distinguished clearly from the latter, either by placing the abbreviation cv. before the cultivar name, or by some typographic device, preferably by enclosing it within single quotation marks.

It should not be printed in italics. When a cultivar name precedes a common name it may be distinguished by a typographical device, preferably by enclosing it within single quotation marks, or it may be used without any particular distinction, provided there is no likelihood of confusion. When a cultivar name is used apart from a botanical or common name, it may be treated as in the preceding case or it may follow the abbreviation cv.

In languages in which capital letters are used, these are required for the initial letter of all words of a cultivar name, except when linguistic usage demands otherwise.

A cultivar name should be attached to a common name only if the common name is unambiguous.

Examples: *Chamaecyparis lawsoniana* cv. Silver Queen, *Chamaecyparis lawsoniana* 'Silver Queen', cv. Silver Queen, 'Silver Queen' or Silver Queen; *Foeniculum vulgare* var. *azoricum* cv. Perfektion, *Foeniculum vulgare* var. *azoricum* 'Perfektion', cv. Perfektion, 'Perfektion' or Perfektion; potato cv. Duke of York, potato 'Duke of York', 'Duke of York' potato, Duke of York potato, cv. Duke of York, 'Duke of York' or Duke of York.

Syringa vulgaris 'Mont Blanc' and lilac 'Mont Blanc' are correct; syringa 'Mont Blanc' and 'Mont Blanc' syringa are incorrect as syringa is the English name for *Philadelphus*, and *Syringa* is also the botanical name for lilac.

Note. Double quotation marks or the abbreviation var. must not be used to distinguish cultivar names.

Article 30

On and after 1 January 1959, a new cultivar name should preferably consist of one or two words and must not consist of more than three words. For the purposes of this Article an arbitrary sequence of letters, an abbreviation, or a numeral is counted as a word (see Rec. 31A).

Article 31

On or after 1 January 1959, new cultivar names in the following form are invalidly published (see Art. 37).

a. The botanical or common name of a genus or the common name of a species if it would lead to confusion.

Examples: Cultivar names such as poplar 'Eucalyptus', camellia 'Rose', and plum 'Apricot' can no longer be validly published since they could be carelessly referred to as eucalyptus 'Poplar', rose 'Camellia', and apricot 'Plum', respectively. However, there is no objection to *Achillea millefolium* 'Rose Queen', carnation 'Ashington Apricot', or carnation 'Heather Pink' since the likelihood of confusion is negligible.

b. The names of cultivars of hybrid origin formed by combining parts of the Latin epithets of the parent species.

Examples: 'Salujapica' must not be used as a cultivar name for a hybrid between *Camellia japonica* and *C. saluenensis* (see also Art. 15).

c. Names including the word variety (or var.) or the word form. However, when var. denotes variegated, the name is not rejected but the word is written in full.

Examples: *Polygonum affine* 'Lowndes' Variety' or *Polygonum affine* 'Lowndes' Var.', *Iris chrysographes* 'Inshriach Form'. *Astrantia major* 'Sunningdale Var.' is expanded to *Astrantia major* 'Sunningdale Variegated'. *Anthemis tinctoria* 'Perry's Variety' was published before 1 January 1959 and must not be shortened to *Anthemis tinctoria* 'Perry'.

Recommendation 31A

It is strongly recommended that, whenever possible, new cultivar names in the following form should be avoided:

a. Names composed of abbreviations, numerals or arbitrary sequences of letters except as established custom in a country or for a crop requires. Example of a crop where such names are admissible: sugar cane 'POJ2878'.

b. Names containing an initial article, unless required by linguistic custom. Examples: Not 'The Colonel' but 'Colonel'; on the other hand, not 'Rochelle' but 'La Rochelle'.

c. Names derived from proper names containing abbreviations, except for the abbreviation 'Mrs.' in English.

Examples: Not 'G. Creelman' but 'George Creelman'; not 'Wm. Thomas' but 'William Thomas'; not 'Mt. Kisco' but 'Mount Kisco'; not 'St. Tudy' but 'Saint Tudy'.

d. Names containing forms of address, unless required by national custom, for example for married women.

Examples: Forms of address to be avoided include Fräulein, Herr, Mademoiselle, Miss, Mister, Monsieur, Señor, Señorita, and equivalents in other languages. Acceptable forms of address include Frau, Madame, Mrs., Señora, and equivalents in other languages, for married women.

e. Names consisting of, or containing, excessively long words or phrases.

Examples: 'Centenaire de Rozain-Bourcharlat'; 'Diplomgartenbauinspektor'.

f. Names exaggerating the merits of a cultivar or which may become inaccurate through the introduction of new cultivars or other circumstances.

Examples: tomato 'Earliest of All'; bean 'Longest Possible'; *Laburnum* 'Latest and Longest'.

g. Names that refer to some attribute or attributes common or likely to become common in a group of related cultivars; on the other hand, names which, while referring to an attribute or attributes, are nevertheless distinctive are acceptable.

Examples: Not rose 'Yellow' but rose 'Yellow Queen'; not endive 'Curled' but endive 'Curly Snowman'; not apple 'Crimson Cooker' but apple 'Crimson Bramley'.

h. Names likely to be confused with existing names within the same or a closely related cultivar class (see Art. 50).

Examples: 'Beatrice' and 'Beatrix'; 'Charmian' and 'Charmain'; 'Ellen', 'Helen', 'Helena', and 'Hélène'; 'Werner', 'Verner', 'Warner', and 'Warnaer'; 'Darwin' and 'Charles Darwin'.

i. Names including the words Cross, Crosses, Hybrid, Hybrids or grex.

j. Names incorporating the common name of the plant.

Examples: Kungsroggen; Aobakomugi.

Recommendation 31B

When a cultivar name is published it should be made clear as to whether or not a breeder, station or brand name is an integral part of the cultivar name.

Note. In some countries legislation forbids the use of the name of a breeder, station or brand as part of a cultivar name since these are held to hinder free marketing of a cultivar after the expiry of its period of protection.

Article 32

When a cultivar name has to be rendered in another language, it is preferably left unchanged. It may, however, be transliterated or translated, in which case the transliteration or translation is regarded as the original name in a different form and its date is that of the original.

Examples: Cucumber 'Noa's Forcing' is a translation of Gurke 'Noas Treib'; Savoy cabbage 'Eisenkopf' is translated into English as 'Ironhead', into French as 'Tête de Fer', into Swedish as 'Järnhuvud'.

'Amanogawa', the name of a cultivar of *Prunus serrulata*, is a transliteration into Roman script from Japanese script.

Recommendation 32A

Personal names should not be translated.

Examples: 'Charles' should not be altered to 'Karl' or 'Karel'; 'San Pietro' should not be altered to 'Saint Peter', 'Sankt Peter', or 'Saint Pierre'; 'Jean Jacques' should not be altered to 'John James'.

20

It is desirable that registration authorities should use one system of transliteration only in respect of any particular language.

PUBLICATION AND USE OF CULTIVAR NAMES

Definitions

Article 33.

A legitimate cultivar name is one in accordance with the Articles of this Code, or one established by legal process, such as entry in a statutory cultivar register, irrespective of any Article of this Code except Art. 42.

An illegitimate cultivar name is one contrary to the Articles of this Code, unless it was established by legal process as provided for above.

The correct name of a cultivar is the earliest legitimate name available except as provided otherwise (see Arts. 27, 44-52).

Note 1. The concept of legitimacy is as defined above. It does not mean in conformity with the law of any particular country. It is possible that a cultivar name may be legitimate in accordance with this Code but not in conformity with particular restrictive legislation.

Note 2. Cultivar names contrary to a Recommendation are not, on that account, illegitimate.

Article 34

In order to be legitimate, cultivar names given before 1 January 1959 must either be validly published according to Arts. 37, 41 and 42, or have been accepted by a registration authority (see Arts. 53–56).

In order to be legitimate, cultivar names published on or after 1 January 1959 must be validly published in accordance with Arts. 37–42.

Article 35

Each cultivar has one correct cultivar name, the single name by which it is internationally known. It may also have one or more legitimate synonyms. A commercial synonym is an alternative name of a cultivar which may be used instead of its correct name under restricted particular circumstances, for instance when a name is commercially unacceptable in a particular country.

Examples: A name is not commercially acceptable when it is difficult to pronounce, or when the original name, or a translation, would have an undesirable connotation or implication.

Recommendation 35A

It is highly desirable that only one cultivar name for a single cultivar should be current under any particular circumstances.

21

Valid Publication

Article 36

In order to be validly published, a cultivar name must be formed in concordance with Arts. 27–31.

Note. In this Code, unless otherwise indicated by the context, the word publication means valid publication.

Article 37

In order to be valid, publication of a cultivar name is effected by the distribution or availability to the public of printed or similarly duplicated matter.

Note 1. For the purpose of this Article, printed or similarly duplicated matter is defined as reading matter multiplied by any mechanical or graphic process whereby a number of identical, legible, indelible copies are made from the original. Microforms and photocopies are included, but hand-written material, even though reproduced by mechanical or graphic processes, and nontechnical newspapers are excluded, except as provided for under Note 2.

Note 2. Chinese, Japanese and Korean books are considered as validly published if, prior to 1 January 1900, they were copied by hand from a hand-written original, or if, before, on or after this date, they were reproduced by mechanical or graphic processes from a hand-written original.

Recommendation 37A

Copies of printed or similarly duplicated matter containing new cultivar names should be sent to the appropriate registration authorities and to suitable libraries.

Article 38

On and after 1 January 1959, for valid publication, the printed or similarly duplicated matter containing the new cultivar name must be clearly dated at least as to year. New cultivar names in undated trade catalogues are validly published only if such catalogues were issued before 1959.

Note. If a trade catalogue is issued unchanged in successive years except for a separately inserted date, it is treated as a single publication with the date of its first issue.

Article 39

In order to be valid, the publication of a cultivar name on or after 1 January 1959 must be accompanied by a description or by a reference to a previously published description as a cultivar or in any botanical category (see Art. 27); for cultivar names published before 1 January 1959, a description or a reference to a previously published description is not necessary.

Recommendation 39A

The description should, when possible, contain particulars to distinguish the cultivar from related cultivars or, when this cannot be done, to place the cultivar in an accepted classification if available. Parentage and history of the cultivar concerned, and name of originator or introducer should be stated when known (see Art. 55).

Recommendation 39B

Whenever possible an illustration should be provided with the description.

When appropriate a preserved specimen and/or an illustration, preferably coloured, should be deposited in a public herbarium and be cited in the description.

Article 40

Any language may be used for the description required for valid publication.

Recommendation 40A

It is recommended that, if a cultivar description is in a language not using Latin or Cyrillic script, a translation or summary of the cultivar description be provided in a language using one of these scripts.

Article 41

Publication of a cultivar name is not valid if against the expressed wish of its originator or his assignee (see Art. 55).

Article 42

A cultivar name is not validly published and must be rejected if the cultivar of which it purports to be the name neither does nor did exist.

Priority

Article 43

The naming of cultivars is based on priority of publication except when expressly limited (see Arts. 27, 44–52).

Article 44

The starting point of valid publication of cultivar names is treated as beginning as follows:

a. From a list designated by an international registration authority (see Art. 53).

b. When no international registration authority exists, from a publication adopted by the International Commission for the Nomenclature of Cultivated Plants after consultation with appropriate organizations.

c. In the absence of such an approved publication, from Philip Miller's *The Gardeners Dictionary*, Ed. 6, 1752.

Note. This edition of Miller's work is the first comprehensive treatment of cultivated plants immediately preceding Linnaeus' *Species Plantarum*, Ed. 1, 1753.

Article 45

The date of a cultivar name is:

a. Before 1 January 1959, that of its valid publication or of its registration, the earlier date taking precedence.

b. On and after 1 January 1959, that of its valid publication.

Article 46

When a cultivar name is generally used instead of any earlier legitimate name of the same cultivar, the former is retained as the correct name if the use of the latter would lead to confusion. If a registration authority exists, such action may be taken only with its approval (see also Art. 27c).

Retention and Re-use of Cultivar Names

Article 47

A cultivar name must remain unchanged when the botanical name is changed (for example, by union or division of genera or by adoption of an earlier name), unless the same cultivar name is already in use in the new position for a different cultivar (see also Arts. 48 and 50).

Example: The following names all refer to the same cultivar: *Scilla hispanica* 'Rose Queen', *S. campanulata* 'Rose Queen', *S. hispanica* var. *campanulata* 'Rose Queen', *Hyacinthoides hispanica* 'Rose Queen', and *Endymion hispanicus* 'Rose Queen'. The cultivar name 'Rose Queen' is unaffected by changes in the nomenclature of the species.

Article 48

The name of a cultivar may not normally be re-used later for any other cultivar. Exceptionally, at the discretion of an international registration authority, re-use of a cultivar name may be authorized, but only if the registration authority is satisfied that the original cultivar is no longer in cultivation, has ceased to exist as breeding material or in a gene or seed bank, and is not an important component in the pedigree of other cultivars.

Rejection of Cultivar Names

Article 49

A cultivar name is to be rejected if it is contrary to the Articles of this Code.

Article 50

Not more than one cultivar may have the same name within the same cultivar class.

Note 1. By cultivar class is meant the taxonomic unit, or assemblage of taxonomic units, within which the use of a cultivar name for two distinct cultivars would lead to confusion. It can correspond, for example, to one or more genera, species, subspecies, or cultivar groups.

Note 2. The limits of a cultivar class are those fixed by an international registration authority, or failing this, by the International Commission for the Nomenclature of Cultivated Plants.

Article 51

When confusion is caused by the use of the same name for two or more widely grown cultivars in the same cultivar class (see Art. 50), the cultivar for which it is the legitimate name is the one selected by a registration authority, or failing this, the cultivar first chosen and published as legitimately bearing the name, or failing this, the cultivar to which the name is most generally applied (see also Arts. 46 and 48).

Note. If a name has been applied legitimately to more than one cultivar within a cultivar class, for example by legal process in different countries, its application should be made precise by addition of an explanatory phrase.

Article 52

The name of a cultivar must be rejected if, owing to an error, it includes a word indicating that the plant concerned belongs to a group to which the cultivar is unrelated.

Example: Cherry 'Kochs Verbesserte Ostheimer' is not related to the Ostheimer group and should therefore be known by the next oldest name, 'Podbielski'.

CULTIVAR REGISTRATION

Article 53

Cultivar registration is the acceptance of a cultivar name by a cultivar registration authority and the inclusion of this name in a register.

A nonstatutory cultivar registration authority is any organization or agency entrusted with registration by agreement of organizations interested. It may be international or national.

A statutory cultivar registration authority is a body responsible for cultivar registration established by legal enactment of a particular country, or by legal agreement between countries.

Registration of trade marks which may be applied to cultivars is a legal process and is not the concern of this code.

Note. Acceptance of a name for cultivar registration does not necessarily imply judgment on the distinctness of the cultivar from others, or on its agricultural, horticultural, or silvicultural merit. The testing of cultivars for distinctness is, nevertheless, of the greatest importance and should, when possible, be carried out before a name is accepted for cultivar registration, as is done for agricultural and other crops in many countries. When publishing lists of registered names, it is desirable that the cultivar registration authorities should indicate clearly whether or not the cultivars concerned have been subject to testing.

Article 54

A name registered by a nonstatutory cultivar registration authority is legitimate only if it conforms with the Articles of this Code.

Article 55

On and after 1 January 1959, a cultivar name must not be listed in a nonstatutory register against the expressed wish of the originator or his assignee.

Note. The originator, in general, is the breeder or discoverer of the cultivar.

Article 56

In countries where trade-marks are also applied to cultivars, they may be entered in nonstatutory cultivar registration lists against the name of the cultivar to which they have been attached. Such trade marks must not be listed against the expressed wish of the trade-mark holder. They should be clearly indicated by the sign ®.

MODIFICATION OF THE CODE

Article 57

This Code may be modified only by action of the International Commission for the Nomenclature of Cultivated Plants of the International Union of Biological Sciences.

APPENDIX

Recommendations for the Guidance of Registration Authorities

1. Registration authorities should require that names submitted for registration be accompanied by the following particulars:

a. The name and address of the originator, the introducer, if any, or their assignees.

b. The name of the describer or namer when the cultivar has been previously described or named, together with a full reference to the date and place of publication.

c. The original name if the name submitted for registration is a commercial synonym.

d. The parentage when known.

e. Particulars of tests for distinctness, including date and place of testing.

f. If awards are mentioned, their date.

g. A description, if no description has already been published.

2. Registration authorities should compile and publish full lists of cultivar names. These lists should, if possible, include:

a. The names of the cultivars in cultivation (see also Art. 56), giving, where available, for each name the particulars enumerated under 1.

b. The names of cultivars which, although no longer cultivated, are of historical importance, for example, as ancestors of existing cultivars.

c. All known synonyms, indicating commercial synonyms as such.

d. Rejected cultivar names

INDEX

References are to Articles and Recommendations

Corn, 11, 26
Correct cultivar name, 33, 35
+*Crataegomespilus*, 8, 23, 24
Crataegus, 23
×*Crataemespilus*, 23
Cross, 18A, 31A
Cucumber, 32
Cultivar class, 31A, 50
Cultivar, definition, 10, 11
Cultivar epithet, 27
×*Cupressocyparis*, 9, 16
Cupressus, 16
Cv., abbreviation of cultivar, 29
Cynodon, 11
Cypress, 16, 29
Cytisus, 21, 23

Description of cultivar, 39, 40
Dianthus, 10
Distinctness of cultivars, 53

Endive, 31A
Endymion, 47
Exaggeration in cultivar names, 31A

Fagus, 3
Festuca, 14
Foeniculum, 29
Form, 25, 31
Forma, 25
Forms of address, 31A
Formula of graft-chimaeras, 20, 21, 24
Formula of hybrids, 13, 14
Fraxinus, 11
French bean, 26

Genus 3, 7, 8, 16, 23, 31, 50
Glycine, 12A
Graft-chimaeras, 2, 8, 9, 11, 20-24
Grex, 18A, 18B, 31A
Group, 12, 26, 50
Growth-habit cultivars, 11

Hawthorn, 23
Heather, 28
Helianthus, 3
Heliocereus, 27
×*Heliochia*, 27
Hemerocallis, 27

Herbarium specimens, 39C
Hibiscus, 27, 28
Hinshu, equivalent of cultivar, 10
Hollyhock, 3
Hordeum, 3
Hyacinthoides, 47
Hybrids, 8-9, 11-19, 23, 31A

Illustration of cultivars, 39B, 39C
Intergeneric hybrids, 8, 13, 14, 16, 17
International Code of Botanical Nomenclature, 2, 10, 13, 17, 25
International Commission for the Nomenclature of Cultivated Plants, 44, 50, 57
Interspecific hybrids, 9, 13, 14, 15, 17, 19
Introducer of a cultivar, 39A, Appendix
Iris, 25, 31

Japanese hand-written books, 37
Jerusalem artichoke, 3
Juglans, 3

Korean hand-written books, 37

+*Laburnocytisus,* 23
Laburnum, 21, 23, 31A
Laelia, 16
Latin names, 2, 10, 13, 15, 17, 27-28
Law and its relation with the Code, 5, 33, 51, 53, 56
Legitimacy, 33, 34, 54
Length of cultivar name, 30, 31A
Lilac, 9, 11, 21, 29
Lilium, 8, 9, 12, 15, 18A, 18B, 28
Lime, 9
Line, 11
Lolium, 11, 14, 26
Lucerne, 11
Lycopersicon, 31A

Maize, 11, 26
Male and female signs, 14A
Malus, 3, 12, 26, 28, 31A
Medicago, 11
Mespilus, 23
Misleading cultivar names, 31A
Modification of the Code, 57
Multiplication sign, 14-16

Nicotiana, 10, 14
Nopalxochia, 27
Numerals in cultivar names and collective epithets, 18, 30, 31A